A Year in the Garden

A Year in the Garden

in England, Wales and Northern Ireland

Photographs by Nick Meers

and Stephen Robson

Text by John Sales

and Margaret Willes

Harry N. Abrams, Inc., Publishers

First published in Great Britain in 2001 by
National Trust Enterprises Ltd.,
36 Queen Anne's Gate, London SW1H 9AS
www.nationaltrust.org.uk/bookshop

Distributed in 2001 by Harry N. Abrams, Incorporated, New York

British Library Cataloguing in Publication Data
A catalogue record for this book is available from the British Library

ISBN 0 7078 0291 1
ISBN 0-8109-6731-6 (Abrams)

Picture research by Margaret Willes
Designed and typeset by Peter and Alison Guy
Production management by Bob Towell
Printed and bound in China
Phoenix Offset

Frontispiece:
Interior of the gardeners' tool shed at
Hidcote Manor Garden in Gloucestershire. [NM]

Introduction

This book will take you through the seasons in a variety of National Trust gardens, from drifts of snowdrops at Anglesey Abbey through the vivid colours of summer and autumn to snow-covered statues at Polesden Lacey. We have tried to include as many gardens as possible, from small town gardens such as Mompesson House in Salisbury and Peckover in Wisbech, to great landscape gardens, such as Stourhead and Bodnant.

There are omissions, and you may be surprised by some of them: perhaps the most famous Trust garden, Sissinghurst Castle, is represented only in details. This is partly because of the fame of Sissinghurst, which gets so many visitors at certain times of the year that the National Trust has on occasion to limit entry. But just as the Trust has many mansions, so it looks after nearly two hundred fine gardens, and we hope that we may have introduced you to some which are not familiar: they are all well worth visiting.

Another factor in our selection has been that we are focusing on the work of two photographers, Nick Meers and Stephen Robson. They have both been providing wonderful images for the National Trust's Photographic Library for many years, and at the back of this book they give some of the technical details of the film and cameras they use. Nick Meers has pioneered the use of panoramic cameras in gardens, while Stephen Robson is now photographing details of plants and flowers. In a book of this size the variety shown can only be limited, but we have tried to feature some unusual plants.

The one element that is missing from all the pictures in the body of the book is people – no distractions allowed from the beauty of the gardens and their plants. This is a paradox, of course, because the garden is the supreme example of the work of people for people, of nature trained by those who design and lay out, and by those who maintain, develop and renew. We pay tribute to creators of some of the world's finest gardens for the breadth of their vision: Henry Hoare at Stourhead; the Batemans and Edward Cooke at Biddulph Grange; Huttleston Broughton at Anglesey Abbey; and the Heathcoat-Amorys at Knightshayes, to name but a few.

Above: Nick Brooks, the head gardener, clipping the Irish yews in the Long Walk at Hinton Ampner in Hampshire. [SR]

Left: Lindy van Creveld, one of the gardeners at Sissinghurst Castle in Kent, pruning the pleached lime trees. [SR]

Gardens never stand still, and the National Trust has been conserving, developing, recreating and restoring gardens ever since Lawrence Johnston bequeathed his world famous garden at Hidcote Manor in 1947. With the guidance first of Graham Stuart Thomas, then myself, John Sales, and my colleagues, and now Mike Calnan and his advisory team, the strands of this developing expertise have been progressively woven into the Trust's work. The National Trust quickly learned that gardening by committee is unsuccessful but there need to be checks and balances: the gardens are too important to be left to the whim of individuals. Over time, the Trust has developed a system by which the local, day-to-day observations and initiative of the gardeners are balanced by the broader perspective and fresh approach of the garden adviser. For important decisions, the Trust draws on the views of a representative of the donor family or advice on aesthetic and historical aspects from its Historic Buildings Department.

The first historical recreation was the garden at Moseley Old Hall. Here Graham Stuart Thomas and Christopher Wall took as their inspiration the designs by Rev. Stonehouse for his garden in Yorkshire laid out in the 1640s, and features to be seen in sixteenth- and seventeenth-century gardening books, such as Thomas Hill's *Gardener's Labyrinth*. The Trust continues to undertake historical recreations, but increasingly has used archaeological investigation with documentary evidence to ensure as much accuracy as possible. The Trust has, for instance, learned a lot in the twenty-five years between its restoration of the early eighteenth-century, Dutch-style garden at Westbury Court and that of the extraordinary Victorian garden at Biddulph Grange.

Just as the National Trust is known as an organisation that conserves the contents of historic houses, so it now plays a major role in the conservation of rare species and historic varieties of plants, flowers and fruit. Graham Stuart Thomas was in the vanguard of this aspect of the Trust's work with the establishment of the collection of Old Roses at Mottisfont Abbey. Given the current popularity of old varieties of roses, it seems inconceivable that they were ever an endangered group, but this was the case. For thirty years the Trust has been involved in the conservation of traditional varieties of fruit and vegetables: perhaps most notably of apples. More recently, orchards growing traditional, local apples have been established around England, and Apple Days introduced by the charity Common Ground are

Fritillaries at Sissinghurst, photographed in April. *Left*: *F. michailovskyi*. *Right*: *F. pyrenaica*. [SR]

The Sunken Parterre, viewed from the Long Gallery at Hanbury Hall in Worcestershire. The parterre was recreated in 1993 to the designs provided *c*.1700 by the gardener George London. [NM]

now popular features of the National Trust's annual calendar.

In its gardens, viewed as a whole, the Trust owns the greatest collection of cultivated plants in the world, some species being scarce and even extinct in their native habitats. The cultural value, historic importance and genetic diversity of this collection is difficult to measure without knowing its full nature and extent. A computerised catalogue is the elusive goal and this is well on the way to being assembled.

Walled kitchen gardens have become a popular part of the visitor route, mirroring the attraction of the 'below stairs' areas in historic houses. By their very nature walled gardens make good car parks, and the Trust has been criticised for its aptitude for this kind of conversion. The Trust is not a vandal by choice; it was the sheer cost and labour intensity of kitchen gardening that dictated these decisions. Luckily, comparatively few were lost in this way, and now every effort is being made to reverse this trend, as shown by the splendid kitchen gardens at Felbrigg Hall and at Beningbrough Hall. But at Beningbrough, for instance, the great nineteenth-century head gardener Thomas Foster had a considerable labour force. So the National Trust, with its limited budgets and what Graham Stuart Thomas called the 'slender work force' has had to modify and adapt in order to manage these gardens and sustain their high standards. But now, thanks to the Heritage Lottery Fund, the National Trust is about to realise its long-held ambition to restore a great walled kitchen garden, complete with all its traditional skills and practices, and to run it as it was in its heyday. This will be at Tatton Park, in association with the tenant, Cheshire County Council.

There are two ways in which the Trust is seeking to remedy the slenderness of the work force. The first is by harnessing the skills and enthusiasm of volunteers. The second is by providing training for young gardeners, following in the best horticultural traditions. The National Trust runs its own three-year training scheme for aspiring gardeners, which combines practical tutelage under some of the most highly-skilled head gardeners in the world, with block release at college: an ideal blend of principles and practice. The only limiting factor, as ever, is funding.

But enough about hard work. Sit back and enjoy the fruits of all these labours, and watch the gardens as they unfold through the year.

John Sales and Margaret Willes
May 2000

The gardeners' shed at Trengwainton Garden in Cornwall: the ceiling is decorated with the prizes won. [NM]

Drifts of snowdrops under a chestnut tree at ANGLESEY ABBEY in Cambridgeshire (*left*). Every year the garden is open to the public for weekends in February so that visitors can admire the magnificent display.

These date back to a discovery made in the 1960s by the head gardener, Richard Ayres. On a rubbish tip that had served the Victorian garden, he found bulbs of an early snowdrop with bright green leaves, thought at first to be *Galanthus transcaucasicus* syn. *G. lagodechianus* but now regarded as a hybrid peculiar to Anglesey Abbey. Together with other distinctive forms it flourishes in large drifts alongside its native cousin, *G. nivalis*. Under the trees and shrubs they can enjoy the light summer shade once the leaves have died down. To maintain their vigour, clumps of plants are lifted, divided, and planted 'in the green' after flowering in March and early April. [NM]

'Lode Star' is the name given at Anglesey Abbey (in the village of Lode) to a particularly fine mid-season form of *Galanthus elwesii*, a large snowdrop with broad, glaucous leaves (*far right*). The species is variable depending on its original location in the wild where it is distributed eastwards from the Pyrenees to the Ukraine, especially in northern Greece and in Turkey.

Right: 'Richard Ayres' (*above*) and 'Ailwyn' (*below*), named respectively after the head gardener and the current Lord Fairhaven, are two outstanding snowdrop cultivars. They have arisen from a liaison between the double form of the native *G. nivalis* and the broad-leaved *G. elwesii* from the Caucasus. [SR]

Camellias bringing early colour to the garden at LANHYDROCK in Cornwall (*left*). The house is tucked into a wooded ridge, facing east down a valley, away from the prevailing winds. The garden slopes to the north, with a cooler and more even microclimate than that of the famous Cornish coastal gardens such as Trelissick and Glendurgan, but still sufficiently benign to encourage early flowering of the camellias. Indeed, the mild winters of recent years have brought the flowering season forward to January which has enabled the National Trust to open its Cornish gardens ahead of the conventional visitor season.

Unusually, much of the garden at Lanhydrock lies above the silvery-grey, granite house, which looks deceptively ancient. In fact, most of the seventeenth-century house was destroyed in a fire in 1881, and rebuilt in a traditional style by the 2nd Baron Robartes, who also laid out the formal 'front' garden.

Right: The informal parts of the garden were laid out in the 1930s by his son, 7th Viscount Clifden, with plantings of camellias, magnolias and rhododendrons which have been augmented by the National Trust over the past forty years. Here, one of the many Himalayan tree magnolias, *M. campbellii* subsp. *mollicomata*, is glimpsed through the trunk of an old field maple. [NM]

Above: Early spring in TRELISSICK GARDEN. Trelissick lies on the south Cornish coast, on the banks of the River Fal, and like many Cornish gardens, it has steep woodlands running down to the shore, which allow frost to 'drain' away to the sea.

In 1937 Trelissick was inherited by Ida Copeland. With her husband, Ronald, she developed and extended the Victorian garden, taking advantage of the mild and moist Cornish climate to plant a garden of great variety. This view is across the main lawn where Japanese maples and the startling shrimp-pink young foliage of *Acer pseudoplatanus* 'Brilliantissimum' create the setting for a garden bench. In the background is a pink *Magnolia campbellii*.

Magnolia campbellii was introduced back in 1865 and when it flowered, many years later, its enormous blossoms must have created a sensation. The pink forms grow well in the mildest gardens, like ANTONY in Cornwall, given shelter for its easily damaged flowers (*left*). [SR]

The famous garden at NYMANS in Sussex has been developed by three generations of the Messel family. Ludwig Messel, from a German Jewish family, came to London in the 1860s, took an English wife, Annie Cussans, and set up a stockbroking firm. In 1890 he bought the estate of Nymans on the Sussex Weald, and with his head gardener, James Comber, began to create the garden.

When Ludwig died in 1916, his son Leonard took over, continuing to subscribe to shares in every important plant-hunting expedition, a garden tradition that has been maintained to the present day. In this way, working closely with Comber, he accumulated an enviable plant collection, especially of magnolias, camellias, rhododendrons and hydrangeas; greatly supplemented when Harold Comber, James's son, was despatched to South America and Tasmania to collect for the garden. The gardening tradition was continued by the third generation of the family, Anne Messel, whose second husband, Michael, was 6th Earl of Rosse.

Although best known perhaps for *Eucryphia × nymansensis* 'Nymansay', magnolias are a Nymans speciality. The photograph above shows two magnificent specimens of *Magnolia campbellii* (Raffillii group) 'Charles Raffill' with the house in the background.

Right: Many of the hybrids developed by Leonard were given family names: M. 'Anne Rosse' (*below left*), M. 'Michael Rosse' (*below right*) and M. × *loebneri* 'Leonard Messel' (*above right*). M. 'Cecil Nice' (*above left*) was named after the head gardener who succeeded James Comber. [SR]

Left: The Wall Garden at NYMANS in early spring. An urn commemorating Leonard's son, Oliver Messel, the theatrical designer, stands in the grass, amid a carpet of daffodils.

A wide variety of bulbs is grown at Nymans: first, snowdrops, snowflakes (*Leucojum*) and crocuses; then, daffodils, fritillaries and erythroniums (see next page). According to the head gardener, David Masters, whatever the bulb, it is grown in the Messel way, naturalised in grass or among shrubs and herbaceous perennials. Daffodils were first planted by the Messels in the 1920s; for example, 'King Alfred', 'Unsurpassable' and 'Cheerfulness'.

Right: Crocuses planted in the Lime Walk, growing in acid, sandy loam. Good cultivars for these conditions include *C. vernus* 'Jeanne d'Arc' (white), 'Pickwick' (striped purple and white), and 'Remembrance' (purple). These are some of the many so-called Dutch hybrids derived from this variable species which is widely distributed throughout the mountainous areas of Southern Europe. [SR]

Overleaf: *Fritillaria meleagris* in the Wall Garden at Nymans. The Dutch seventeenth-century obsession with the tulip – 'tulipomania' – is well known. The fritillary was held with equal fascination, even though such large sums may not have been spent on purchasing its bulbs. The mysterious purple snakeshead is celebrated in paintings and on Delft tiles of the period, alongside the exotic tulip. Normally fritillaries are associated with damp, open grassland and are natives of the water meadows of the Thames Valley. But at Nymans they flourish in light, acid greensand, even under trees. Here they are planted with *Erythronium californicum* 'White Beauty', one of the easiest erythroniums to grow, even in limey soils. [SR]

The Dell lies at the heart of the garden at TRELISSICK – damp, humid and sheltered. Here flourish exotic tree rhododendrons, uncommon hydrangea species, New Zealand tree ferns, tender bamboos and a banana, all underplanted with ferns, astilbes, primulas, cimicfugas, willow gentians and the Japanese *Kirengeshoma palmata*.

Ferris's Cottage is named after Ernie Ferris, one of the gardeners who worked at Trelissick. It is now a National Trust holiday cottage. [SR]

COLETON FISHACRE is situated on a peninsula formed by the River Dart in Devon, enjoying mild winters and hot summers. The estate was bought in 1923 by Rupert, son of Richard D'Oyly Carte of Gilbert & Sullivan fame, with the money from the hugely successful Savoy operas. His wife Lady Dorothy, a keen gardener, laid out the gardens with the help of a pupil of Sir Edwin Lutyens, the architect, Oswald Milne, whose hand can be seen in the formal terracing around the house.

Below the formal terraces, the stream breaks free over the shaly rock to unite the garden with the sound of running water. All along its way, it is exploited to nourish a wide range of moisture-lovers and marginal plants including candelabra primulas, shuttlecock fern and irises. Here Exbury hybrid and common azaleas frame the stream and give fragrance in early May. [SR]

The sheltered, secret valley at
COLETON FISHACRE runs
steeply down to the sea. In the
woodland garden known as
'Newfoundland', native bluebells
grow alongside the white, garlic-
like, *Allium triquetrum*, the
species name referring to its
three-angled stems. [SR]

The Stream Garden at TRENGWAINTON. The name Trengwainton is Cornish for 'the House of the Springs', and many of these springs feed the streams in the garden and keep moist the soil which is acid, medium loam. As with many Cornish coastal gardens, the climate is very mild, warmed by the Gulf Stream, allowing tender exotics to flourish in the shelter of the woodlands and walled garden.

In the early nineteenth century Trengwainton was laid out by Sir Rose Price, using the wealth from his Jamaican sugar plantations. He organised the garden into compartments, the bones of which are still to be seen. The garden was later developed by the Bolitho family, and in particular by Lt Col Sir Edward Bolitho, who gave Trengwainton to the National Trust in 1961.

After the Second World War, it was Sir Edward who had the culvert opened up and the Stream Garden planted to create a scenic drive. His head gardener, George Hulbert, planted masses of candelabra primulas (*Primula japonica* and *P. prolifera*) tree ferns (*Dicksonia antarctica*) and other moisture-loving plants to add another dimension to this delightful woodland garden of magnolias, rhododendrons, camellias and choice tender plants. [NM]

One of the greatest plant collections belonging to the National Trust is to be found at KNIGHTSHAYES COURT in Devon. From 1937, Sir John and Lady Heathcoat-Amory worked on their garden, creating a layout notable as much for the sophisticated discipline of its planting as for the wealth and variety of its collection.

Inheriting a Victorian formal pattern of terraces and hedged compartments, they adapted the layout brilliantly. In the Paved Garden, against the close-clipped yew, is set a soft but regular arrangement of wisterias and dense, low planting with a central cistern. In the beds are erysimums, bergenias and *Allium karataviense*, the Turkestan allium, with its glaucous leaves and ball-shaped flower heads. In the foreground is a terrace of alpine plants. [SR]

The most famous planting at KNIGHTSHAYES is the Garden in the Wood (*left*). This was gradually planted up from the 1950s by Sir John and Lady Heathcoat-Amory, and now consists of 12 hectares (30 acres) of ornamental walks and glades, under a canopy of oaks, beeches, limes and conifers, planted in the 1860s and heavily thinned. These provide a kindly, dappled shade for the understorey planting of shrubs, bulbs and herbaceous plants in carefully contrived but seemingly naturalised plant combinations. Here there are Lenten roses, bluebells and dicentras in the foreground with euphorbias and azaleas behind.

Right: Lenten roses are forms and hybrids of *Helleborus orientalis*, which have been intensively developed in gardens over more than a century and a half. Although there are many named cultivars, now including yellowish tints and double flowers, seedlings can equally well be selected and enjoyed for their varied habit, soft colours and beautiful markings. Through late winter and spring they unfailingly reveal their subtle charm, despite the worst of the weather. [SR]

Left: The Old Castle at SCOTNEY in Kent, looking down from the Bastion over a patchwork of azaleas, rhododendrons, maples and crab apples. The garden at Scotney was created in the 1830s by Edward Hussey with the help of the Rev. William Sawrey Gilpin, nephew of the high priest of the Picturesque movement, William Gilpin. The latter had advocated the idea of a garden resembling a landscape painting, with drama, variety and rough edges. Hussey and Gilpin demolished parts of the moated medieval castle to give it a fairy-tale look, and planted and designed the area around the Bastion to provide contrived, picturesque views. A new comfortable house in the Elizabethan style was designed by Anthony Salvin and sited at the top of the Bastion especially to take advantage of these views of the garden and the park.

In the twentieth century, Hussey's grandson Christopher and his wife Betty developed and enriched the garden to provide a wide array and succession of colour to add to the spectacular groups of spring-flowering, hardy hybrid rhododendrons, Ghent azaleas and kalmias. They planted shrub roses and herbaceous plants for the summer, trees for autumn colour, and a herb garden, designed by Lanning Roper, was sited near the Castle.

Right: Winding paths lead down from the Bastion through the mysterious shade of the quarry, from which Edward Hussey obtained his stone for building the house and terracing. Here the steps are edged with Welsh poppies and ferns, with Ghent azaleas and acers forming a canopy. [SR]

The great landscape garden at STOURHEAD in Wiltshire was primarily the creation of Henry Hoare II, son of the founder of the famous London bank. In 1742 he returned from a grand tour of Italy, his head full of visions of the landscapes of the Roman Campagna. In the following years he worked on the landscape of his estate at Stourton, treating the valley as a canvas on which he would paint a poetic vision. He created lakes and erected temples and eye-catchers against the backdrop of his wooded hillsides. The route from his Palladian house was planned according to the precepts of the emerging eighteenth-century English Landscape style, as a sequence of experiences incorporating a variety of changing views, culminating in the panorama from Apollo's Hill.

This classical landscape was subsequently enriched by his grandson, Sir Richard Colt Hoare, who laid paths so that visitors could enjoy the circuit walk. He began the Hoare tradition of arboretum planting, widening the range of exotic trees and shrubs to include the tulip tree and other recently-introduced species from the New World, as well as cherry laurel and pontic rhododendron.

Successive generations of the Hoare family have made their mark to evolve a complex garden of great beauty and interest throughout the year. In early spring, wild flowers sprinkle the banks of the lakes, as seen in a view across to the Pantheon (*above*). In late spring, there is a burst of colour from the more modern rhododendrons and azaleas as seen in this photograph of the Temple of Apollo (*right*). These shrubs were introduced by Sir Henry Hoare, who gave the property to the National Trust in the mid-twentieth century. [NM]

The Italian Garden at BIDDULPH GRANGE in Staffordshire, looking south towards the Rhododendron Ground. The gardens at Biddulph were created in the mid-nineteenth century by James and Maria Bateman. Just as the Great Exhibition of 1851 celebrated the world's manufacturing achievements, so Biddulph is a reflection of the Victorian fascination with the whole world's flora, then being made accessible by exploration and by improved means of transporting live plants on board ship using the 'Wardian case', a sealed packing case with a glazed roof.

Terraced and stepped gardens based on Italian Renaissance examples became popular in England in the early nineteenth century. The Italian Garden at Biddulph takes the basic concept but adds Victorian overtones, such as ribbon planting in borders on either side of the paved steps. Behind these borders are massed plantings of late flowering rhododendrons. The white *Pieris floribunda* has survived from the Batemans' plantings, though most of the others have been replaced.

This brilliant patchwork of colour flows down to the

Rhododendron Ground, also known as the American Garden. James Bateman was particularly fond of azaleas and rhododendrons, and planted the area with species recently arrived from North America, such as the hardy evergreen *R. catawbiense* from Virginia and *R. maximum*, the 'Great Laurel' or 'Rose Bay' of eastern USA. These were being hybridised with the now ubiquitous *R. ponticum* from Turkey and Iran to produce the first evergreen hardy hybrids, several of which survive at Biddulph, a remarkable snapshot of this period of rhododendron breeding. Also from the original introductions is *R. occidentale*, a fragrant deciduous azalea with creamy-white flowers in July, which was introduced by William Lobb in 1851. At the same time James Bateman was receiving and planting the first Himalayan and Chinese rhododendrons to be made available in England, including *R. falconeri*, *R. fortunei*, *R. ciliatum*, *R. barbatum* and *R. arboreum*. [NM]

Left: A massive stone gateway between the Dragon Parterre and China, perhaps the most famous of the 'national' gardens at BIDDULPH GRANGE. The stonework, of exceptional quality, contrasts with the delicate foliage of a Japanese maple, one of the originals planted by the Batemans. All the architectural features at Biddulph were the result of the Batemans' collaboration with their friend Edward Cooke, a designer and marine painter, to whose fertile imagination the garden owes a great deal.

Exotic plants brought from the Far East were placed in an appropriate setting in China, a willow-pattern plate brought to life with a wooden bridge leading round to a temple painted in gold, green and red (*above*). Many of the plants set here by the Batemans were discovered by the plant hunter, Robert Fortune. The golden larch *Pseudolarix amabilis*, native to China, is the sole survivor of a batch of the first plants of this species ever to be introduced into Britain. As such, it is perhaps botanically the most important tree looked after by the National Trust. In contrast, in the foreground of this picture, is *Rhododendron luteum*, the fragrant pontic azalea from the Caucasus that is now widely grown. [NM]

The Auricula Theatre at CALKE ABBEY, Derbyshire. Auriculas, derived from *Primula auricula*, were brought to Britain by Flemish and Huguenot craftsmen fleeing religious persecution in the sixteenth century. They cherished these flowers for their formal beauty and the variety of their markings, displaying them in wooden staged theatres with a curtain to keep off the strong sun and rain. The theatre in the walled gardens at Calke is a unique survival, built in the 1770s and recently restored in blue and biscuit brown, two colours from the original Calke livery. The auriculas are displayed here during their flowering season between mid-April and the end of May, after which pelargoniums are staged in their place.

The auricula plants are provided by two local growers, Doug Lochhead and Val Woolley. They aim to build up a separate collection for Calke, based on as many different varieties and colours as possible, growing about 1,000 plants to get around 250 in flower at the same time. Three cultivars that appear regularly at Calke are the crimson-red 'Argus', the yellow and green fancy 'Hinton Fields' and the double, dark purple-blue 'Walton Heath'. [SR]

: 44 : The Maze at GLENDURGAN in Cornwall. Glendurgan is a woodland garden on Cornwall's south coast, three valleys converging on the village of Durgan on the Helford estuary. The Fox family developed the garden here from the early nineteenth century, using their contacts as shipping agents to obtain exotic seeds and plants which would flourish in the shelter and mild climate of Glendurgan.

The garden is planted with a remarkable range of rare and tender plants, including rhododendrons and a young olive grove, with woodland gardens rolling down to the river. But in the middle, on a west-facing slope, lies something quite unexpected: a maze of cherry laurel, originally planted by Alfred Fox in 1833, and recently restored by the National Trust. The rare asymmetrical pattern is made up of laurel hedges over three quarters of a mile (1.2 km) long which take two gardeners a week to prune – and they have to do this five times a year! The centre of the maze is marked by a little thatched summer house, designed by Charles Fox who lives in the main house, while Chusan palms (*Trachycarpus fortunei*), transplanted fully grown, provide eye catchers – or possibly markers for lost visitors. [SR]

The Sunken Garden at
HINTON AMPNER in
Hampshire. The estate at
Hinton Ampner was
inherited in 1935 by Ralph
Dutton, who became 8th
Lord Sherborne. A passionate
gardener and author of *The
English Garden*, he devoted
the next fifty years to re-
making the garden around
his manor house.

The Sunken Garden was the
first area he laid out,
approached by an avenue of
Irish yews. The soil is heavy
and alkaline, wet and cold in
winter, hot and dry in
summer. The raised beds
facing south contain a range
of drought-tolerant sun
lovers. In this photograph can
be seen *Euphorbia wulfenii*,
Erysimum 'Bowles' Mauve',
and *Aubrieta deltoidea*. The
beds set into the lawn are
planted with a combination
of tulips to give successive
flowering – 'Arabian Mystery',
'Atlantic' and 'Blue Heron' –
all in similar shade of purple
with white edges. The yew
topiary is cut to resemble
mushroom-shaped 'staddle
stones', traditionally used to
keep rats out of grain stores.
[SR]

Topiary and statuary at CLIVEDEN, Buckinghamshire. The large and elaborate gardens at Cliveden were first laid out in the opening years of the eighteenth century by Lord Orkney, but underwent considerable changes under subsequent owners, notably the Sutherland family in the mid-nineteenth century, and the Astors at the beginning of the twentieth century.

Left: The parterres decorating the lawns below the house were laid out in the 1850s by John Fleming, head gardener to the Duke and Duchess of Sutherland. If Mr Fleming is to be believed, they commemorate a revolution in Victorian gardening. Unlike his predecessors, who resorted to evergreens and bare beds through the autumn, winter and early spring months, he began the practice of bedding out in the autumn with plants and bulbs that would overwinter in the beds and provide a spring display until it was safe to plant frost-tender summer flowers. He recorded this triumph in *Spring and Winter Flower Gardening* published in 1870.

Today the National Trust is obliged to use a less labour-intensive, semi-permanent planting of grey-leaved *Santolina chamaecyparissus* (syn. *S. incana), Brachyglottis* 'Sunshine' and *Nepeta* 'Six Hills Giant', a large catmint. Fleming's edging was of clipped privet and spruce; now there are box hedges and sentinel clipped yews.

Right: The Long Garden was laid out by the lst Viscount Astor to echo the parterres. Around a linear composition of box-edged beds, he set out some of his collection of urns, well heads, statues and sarcophagi. This photograph shows a group of eighteenth-century figures frozen in a stately dance, overlooked by a peacock in yew topiary.

The large beds edged with serpentine clipped box, now containing yuccas and variegated euonymus, were originally giant herbaceous borders, designed by Norah Lindsay. Perhaps the most influential flower gardener of the first half of the twentieth century, Mrs Lindsay had a seemingly instinctive talent for producing subtle colour schemes and flowery effects of great freedom and luxuriance. She was Lawrence Johnston's *alter ego* at Hidcote and her work was much admired by Vita Sackville-West of Sissinghurst. [NM]

Overleaf: The Pool Garden at CHIRK CASTLE, with a bronze nymph modestly emerging. Most of the planting in this informal area was arranged by Lady Margaret Myddelton between 1950 and 1980: left to right, *Cornus florida*, *Acer palmatum* 'Atropurpureum', irises, ferns and hostas. In a recent poll of members, the garden at Chirk was voted the most enjoyed garden in the National Trust. [SR]

Right: The Italian Garden looking towards the north front of BELTON HOUSE, Lincolnshire. Belton House was built in the 1680s for Sir John Brownlow, possibly by Captain William Winde, a military man turned architect. Winde may also have been responsible for the original gardens here; he certainly laid out the terraces at Cliveden and also probably worked on the famous terraced gardens at Powis Castle in Wales. Whoever designed the original gardens at Belton organised a formal scheme that was swept away in the eighteenth century, but recalled by later generations of Brownlows.

The Italian Garden is now arranged on a central sequence of orangery, circular fountain and lion exedra. The last is a Roman garden feature that was revived during the Renaissance: it has a semi-circular stone backdrop, with arched niches. Ornamental pots and urns flank the steps of the Italian Garden and act as exclamation marks, standing out from the low mounds of bedding.

The bedding displays, changed twice each year, follow the colour schemes traditionally favoured by the Brownlow family: red, yellow and blue. In spring, therefore, the beds are planted out with tulips and wallflowers; in summer with pelargoniums, heliotropes, *Helichrysum petiolare* and dahlias, notably 'Bishop of Llandaff' and 'Madame Stappers' (a cultivar particular to certain National Trust properties). This typically Victorian colour scheme is echoed in the ornamental urns, including spectacular displays in the lion exedra, where pots can rest in the arched niches and plinths.

Left: In the West Courtyard, a former fountain head is the setting for striking red *Pelargonium* 'Bruni' and the ivy-leaved *P.* 'L'Elégante'. [NM]

: 54 : The interior of the Orangery at BELTON. Originally built by Jeffry Wyatville in 1810, it was remodelled in the mid-century by the addition of a glass roof, allowing more light for exotic plants. At one stage it was filled with parrots, at another used as the restaurant for the house, but it is once again a sanctuary for plants.

Even without a heating system the Orangery provides enough winter protection for a wide range of tender plants to flourish – camellias, climbers, bulbs and flowering plants. Around the pool the lush effect is brightened with arum lilies and a variegated zonal pelargonium, 'Caroline Schmidt'. [NM]

The garden at TINTINHULL in Somerset was created by Phyllis Reiss between 1933 and 1953. Around the charming eighteenth-century manor house she laid out six rectangular courtyards, separated by high hedges and brick walls. As at Hidcote (pages 68–73), but on a much smaller scale, she was producing a series of 'garden rooms' linked by vistas.

Right: This vista is from the Pool Garden looking into the Kitchen Garden. During Mrs Reiss's time, visitors were not permitted into the kitchen garden: she took the line that vegetables were for eating, not for looking at. Thus the views into the garden were softened by flower borders along the paths planted with ornamentals. The arch is framed by a cabbage relative, *Crambe cordifolia* with the greenish-yellow *Alchemilla mollis* low on the left. In the vegetable garden border, the pink rose 'Mevrouw Nathalie Nypels' can be seen between white valerian and the stately, green umbels of angelica beyond.

Left: Today the Kitchen Garden is open to visitors to view the rows of vegetables, herbs and cut flowers, laid out like a cottage garden. Since 1999, the garden has formed part of the gardens scheme promoted by the Henry Doubleday Heritage Seed Library. Seeds of scarce and old vegetable varieties that have fallen foul of European Union legislation concerning the sale of commercial cultivars are grown here and the crops returned to the Heritage Seed Library for the use of members. Phyllis Reiss's memory lives on in the borders of catmint, *Nepeta* 'Six Hills Giant' which flank the paths. On the right is *Smyrnium perfoliatum* which retains its greenish-yellow colouring even after the seeds have set. [NM]

Left: The magnificent Rose Garden at MOTTISFONT ABBEY in Hampshire was established from 1972 onwards by Graham Stuart Thomas, to conserve varieties of Old Roses. He made use of Mottisfont's walled kitchen garden, retaining the traditional cruciform layout and pattern of paths and box hedges.

Over three hundred varieties have been assembled, almost all of which were raised before 1900. The collection includes species and some very ancient cultivars derived from them.

Above right: *Rosa gallica* 'Officinalis', the Apothecary's Rose, is also known as the Red Rose of Lancaster. In thirteenth-century France it was grown to produce a fragrant powder from its dried pulverised petals.

Above, far right: Rose 'Charles de Mills' is one of the finest of the Gallica group of old hybrid shrub roses, having been bred in 1830. With its intense fragrance it makes an excellent buttonhole.

Below, far right: 'Gloire de Ducher' is a tall Hybrid Perpetual raised in France in 1865. Growing to about 2m (6ft) high it produces the main flush of its richly voluptuous flowers in June, followed by more in late summer and usually a good autumn blooming.

Below, right: China Rose 'Louis XIV'. China roses were bred in Europe in the nineteenth century from ancient Chinese cultivars. The original species *R. chinensis* is rare and has only recently been reintroduced from Yemen. Although often slightly tender, they have provided the bushy repeat flowering character that has become a feature of modern roses. [SR]

Most of the roses at MOTTISFONT flower once in a glorious display that reaches its climax, usually around the middle of June. As well as providing flowers to lengthen the season, herbaceous plants, biennials and ground covers are used between and in front of the roses to give variety of form, foliage colour and texture. Traditional herbaceous borders flanking the central axis are planted with broad drifts of flowering plants to complement the roses and to provide continuous colour and fragrance through the summer. [SR]

Right: The Rose Garden at NYMANS was originally designed by Leonard Messel's wife, Maud, in the 1920s. She had built up a collection of old-fashioned varieties, some given to her by the rosarians Ellen Willmott and Edward Bunyard, and others brought from gardens in France and Italy. As a result Nymans became one of the few gardens where nineteenth-century cultivars, especially hybrid moss roses, survived between the World Wars.

By 1985 most of the roses were tired and suffering from rose sickness and the shadow of trees, while the paths could not take the increasing numbers of visitors to this popular National Trust garden. Based on the original layout, a much larger rose garden was designed by John Sales, the Trust's Head of Gardens, with arches and pillars modelled on those that had survived. At the time of the great storm of 1987 the area was empty and in the process of being regenerated. Despite general chaos of fallen trees, David Masters and the garden staff completed the job to make the Rose Garden the vanguard of the revival of the whole garden. Over 150 cultivars were planted, including some propagated from those surviving from Maud Messel's time.

The pond was redesigned and Vivien ap Rhys Pryce created a fountain in the form of a bronze rose to stand in the centre of the garden, while the paths were edged with geraniums, *G.* 'Johnson's Blue' and *G. clarkei* 'Kashmir White' and 'Kashmir Purple' with *Persicaria affinis* (syn. *Polygonum affine*) 'Superba' and *Nepeta* × *faasenii*.

Left: 'Henri Martin', a red moss rose.
[SR]

SNOWSHILL MANOR in Gloucestershire is one of the Trust's more extraordinary properties. The old manor house was bought in the early twentieth century by Charles Paget Wade, who proceeded to fill it with collections of every kind, from kitchen bygones to Japanese Samurai armour. In time he was obliged to move out of the main house and into the Priest's House next door, managing to live there surrounded by yet more collections.

The garden at Snowshill also contains collections: gate piers, troughs, cisterns and well heads. Wade, an architect by training, believed 'a garden is an extension of the house, a series of outdoor rooms', and created a patchwork of linked enclosures incorporating cunningly contrived contrasts of hardness and softness, floweriness and greenness, intimacy and exposure, light and shade.

Right: This view looks out from the cart shed into the Well Garden. Set up on the wall is a clock in blue and gold, Wade's favoured blue echoing the colour combinations of astronomical clocks produced in the early sixteenth century – an example of which can be seen at Hampton Court Palace.

Left: The gentle sound of trickling water also links the garden's various levels, here emerging from a bronze water spout from C.P. Wade's collection, among roses like 'François Juranville', 'Alchymist' and 'New Dawn' tumbling on the stone walls. [NM]

Right: The house seen down the main vista of topiary yew at PACKWOOD in Warwickshire. The great topiary garden at Packwood is a bit of a mystery. Tradition has it that the yews represent the Sermon on the Mount, with The Master standing on the summit of a mound, 12 Apostles, 4 Evangelists on the terrace, and a lawn filled with the assembled Multitude. A plan drawn in 1732 shows only the yews on the terrace. It seems that the Multitude was planted in the nineteenth century, when the area was replanted as an orchard, and retained when the apple trees were eventually grubbed out. While the origin of the tradition may be in doubt, there is no denying the dignified beauty of the piece.

No mystery surrounds the huge task of keeping this topiary in impeccable shape. Most can be cut safely from an hydraulic platform, but the gardeners at Packwood regard The Master as the most difficult to clip, from ladders set at a seemingly precarious angle, well secured by ropes.

In marked contrast to the impressive formality and restrained colours of the topiary garden, the flower garden is cheerfully bright, with warm colours predominating (*above*). The planting arrangement would have been described in the nineteenth century as the 'mingled, ribbon style', with individual plants and small groups repeated along the length of the borders and graded evenly from front to back. The survival of this style at Packwood, despite the universal popularity of Gertrude Jekyll's 'drifts', can be credited to E.D. Lindup, one of the National Trust's first head gardeners. The borders of the raised terrace form a riot of colour in the summer, with red hot pokers, *Brachyglottis* 'Sunshine', day-lilies, hostas, geraniums and catmint. [SR]

HIDCOTE MANOR GARDEN in Gloucestershire is one of the world's most influential gardens, yet when Lawrence Johnston and his mother, Mrs Winthrop, acquired the manor in 1907, it was surrounded by exposed farmland. Johnston quickly developed an interest in gardening. In response to the site and by trial and error, he established an elaborate asymmetrical network of mostly hedged enclosures using changes of scale, design, planting and style to provide impact and variety. Within this essentially architectural framework of long vistas, hedges, walls and topiary, the planting is exuberantly informal, carefully contrived but apparently spontaneous.

The walled Old Garden comprised the full extent of the garden at Hidcote in 1907, and was the first part that Lawrence Johnston

developed. It underwent several changes even before the vista was opened up through the Circle to the Red Borders and the Stilt Garden. The deep, double-sided borders of shrubs, herbaceous perennials, roses, bulbs and ground covers are planted luxuriantly in big, informal drifts in the Hidcote style. It was probably Norah Lindsay's influence in the 1930s that finally decided the colour scheme of soft blues and pinks, cream, white and pale yellow, with silver foliage. Prominent here in midsummer is the tall *Campanula lactiflora*, and in front the silver *Artemisia ludoviciana*. [NM]

The White Garden at HIDCOTE, seen here in mid-summer, is in fact tiny in scale. The cruciform pattern of beds is edged with box that bursts into topiary birds at the corners. Lawrence Johnston used a variety of different planting schemes here. Now in summer there is the floribunda rose 'Gruss an Aachen', first raised in Germany in 1909. Throughout the summer, its creamy white flowers are overlaid with pale pink. The roses are enhanced by a range of white and silver-leaved plants, including *Crambe cordifolia*, *Lamium maculatum* 'White Nancy', *Artemisia absinthium* 'Lambrook Silver', campanulas, and the double feverfew, *Tanacetum parthenium* 'White Bonnet'. [NM]

Overleaf: The Red Borders at HIDCOTE. In contrast to the pastel colours of the Old Garden, the Red Borders' colour scheme is startling, including all the reds through into orange, accompanied by violet-blue set dramatically against purple foliage. As well as the old floribunda rose 'Frensham' in the foreground, permanent plants include *Lilium pardalinum*, orange day-lilies, grassy *Miscanthus sinensis* 'Gracillimus' and *Buddleja davidii* 'Black Knight'. These are principally summer and early autumn borders, the real excitement coming from tender plants that include dahlias, purple-leafed cannas, cultivars of *Lobelia cardinalis*, *Begonia* 'Hatton Castle', salvias and the scarlet *Verbena* 'Lawrence Johnston'. [NM]

LYTES CARY MANOR in Somerset was the home of Henry Lyte, whose translation of Dodoen's *Cruedeboek* was the first herbal in English, published in 1578. The Tudor house was bought in 1907 by Sir Walter Jenner, son of the famous physician, William.

Jenner recreated the atmosphere of a sixteenth-century garden, with clipped yew topiary leading up to the front door. He laid out the rest of the garden as a series of enclosures, described by Christopher Hussey as 'a necklace of garden rooms strung on green corridors', much restored by the National Trust in the 1960s and '70s. Just as Vita Sackville-West created a White Garden at Sissinghurst Castle, so Jenner designed a much less ambitious garden of white flowers and silver foliage at Lytes Cary.

Above: The White Garden at Lytes Cary is set off well by stone walls and a high clipped yew hedge in contrast to the whites and silvers of the planting. In the border there are mock orange and roses for their fragrance, the double feverfew and the white form of the Dusty Miller – *Lychnis coronaria*. *Ballota pseudodictamnus* also provides silver foliage. [NM]

One of the more spectacular features at Lytes Cary is the main border running along a south-facing wall. This was planted by Sir Walter as a colour sequence in the style made famous by the garden designer, Gertrude Jekyll. When the National Trust renovated the garden after 1963, this border was replanned and enriched. At the far end are the blues and yellows of potentilla, clematis, caryopteris, Jacob's ladder and *Geranium psilostemon*. The colours then begin to hot up, moving through the purples and rich crimsons to pink and light yellow. In the foreground are roses, including *Rosa gallica* 'Versicolor' (syn. *Rosa mundi*) 'Rosemary Rose', *R.* 'Yellow Holstein' and 'Lavender Lassie', set off by the purple smoke bush and in front, catmint and the dark red *Astilbe arendsii* 'Fanal'. [NM]

Although made largely by the National Trust, the garden at ACORN BANK in Cumbria reflects the history of the property. In the Middle Ages, it was a commandery of the Knights Templar, the military order whose original task was to guard the Temple in Jerusalem and provide aid for pilgrims on their travels in the Holy Land.

In 1969 Graham Stuart Thomas suggested that the vacant kitchen garden should provide a home for a comprehensive collection of medicinal and culinary herbs. Many of the herbs are, of course, sun-loving and used to a dry climate, in complete opposition to the cold wet climate of Cumbria. But thanks to the garden being sheltered, south-facing and partly walled, it has proved possible to grow a remarkable range of herbs and medicinal plants in the rich vegetable soil.

Left: This photograph shows the main walled garden at Acorn Bank which has been given over to an orchard. A hedged grass walk with an avenue of double morello cherry runs through it. The orchard grass is allowed to grow long to encourage wild flowers and naturalised flowers: here are ox-eye daisies in early summer. Mown grass paths give access to sumptuous mixed borders against the perimeter walls – white foxgloves, cream aruncus, silver wormwood (*Artemisia absinthum*), purple cotinus, blue catmint, with pink 'Albertine' roses on the wall.

A wide variety of herbs can be found in the former kitchen garden. *Above*: Indian Physic (Bowman's Root) *Gillenia trifoliata* is a charming perennial, elegant enough to grace the flower border quite apart from its medicinal interest. A native of North America, where the Indians and the settlers dried and pulverised the roots as an emetic and for stomach trouble. It is easy to grow and thrives at Acorn Bank. [SR]

Near right: Angelica (*A. archangelica*) is a robust, aromatic, perennial plant with bold leaves that grows up to 1.8m (6ft) bearing large umbels of greenish yellow flowers in July: the seed heads persist on stout hollow stems. It grows easily and is more suitable for semi-wild places than for the border, where self-sown seedlings can be a nuisance. It has been prized for centuries, the stems and seeds being used in confectionery and the powdered roots as a remedy for coughs, colds, pleurisy, wind, colic, rheumatism and diseases of the urinary organs.

Middle right: Woad, *Isatis tinctoria*. A native, it must have been common in ancient times, used by the British, according to the Romans, to stain themselves blue. Dried and ground-up, the leaves were also used widely by the Anglo-Saxons for staining cloth, and woad was cultivated as a crop for this purpose until largely superseded by indigo. A member of the cabbage family, it is usually grown as a biennial, sown in summer to flower the following year between June and September.

Far right: Henbane (*Hyoscaymus niger*) is a poisonous member of Solanaceae, the family of the potato, the tomato, tobacco and belladonna. It is widely distributed naturally, occurring as an annual or biennial throughout central and southern Europe, western Asia and India, often cropping up uninvited in gardens through its seeds being inadvertently included in packing materials or flower seeds. More interesting, even sinister, than beautiful, it has been used for centuries as a narcotic medicine, having antispasmodic, hypnotic and diuretic properties. [SR]

As the *National Trust Guide* has it, 'Polesden Lacey is alive with the spirit of Mrs Ronald Greville'. Maggie Greville was one of the great hostesses of the early twentieth century, friend of King Edward VII and a social lioniser. One of her most arresting remarks was 'One uses up *so* many red carpets in a season!'

The Regency villa of POLESDEN LACEY in Surrey was bought in 1906 as a country home for the Grevilles by Maggie's father, the brewer Willliam McEwan. The house was duly enlarged and enriched, and Captain Greville had plans to do the same with the garden. When he died in 1908, his widow decided to make use of the existing framework of avenues, lawns, walks and walled enclosures.

The main part of the former walled kitchen garden thus became her Rose Garden, with a cross pattern of wooden pergolas to bear the roses, and paths flanked by borders of Munstead and Hidcote lavenders. *Right*: This photograph shows the Lavender Walk with a small statue. Statues and other kinds of garden ornament are scattered throughout the gardens at Polesden Lacey. In the Lavender Garden, for instance, a sundial armillary sphere forms an eye catcher amid various lavender cultivars (*left*). [NM]

A striking feature of the gardens at POLESDEN LACEY is the 'moon windows'. *Left*: This window looks through to the Lavender Garden, focusing on the armillary sphere (see page 80). In the foreground is part of the south-facing herbaceous border which runs the whole length of the formal garden. *Achillea* 'Coronation Gold' contrasts dramatically with *Salvia nemorosa*.

In the opposite direction, another 'moon window' looks from the Iris Garden towards a statue of Diana the Huntress (*above*). [NM]

: 88 : The Dutch Garden at LYME PARK, Cheshire. The formal gardens at Lyme present a dramatic contrast to the wild landscape of the park beyond, high and remote on the edge of the Peak District. The hall itself was originally a hunting lodge, transformed into a classical mansion by the Venetian architect, Giacomo Leoni in the early years of the eighteenth century.

The heyday of the formal gardens at Lyme came in the late nineteenth century; their nadir was reached in 1973 when a high retaining wall collapsed and the Dutch Garden was inundated. Now it is restored to its high Victorian splendour, with an intricate pattern of beds circling out from the central fountain. Each bed, edged with ivy, is filled with seasonal colour: for example, in spring, tulips and forget-me-nots; in summer, scarlet *Lobelia* 'Queen Victoria' and silver *Senecio cineraria* 'White Diamond'. [NM]

Left: The Orangery at
LYME was designed by
Lewis Wyatt in 1815, and
remodelled some fifty years
later by Alfred Darbyshire.
It still contains the fig tree
planted here in Victorian
times, and camellias cover
an entire wall, providing
an unforgettable sight in
spring.

   The sunken parterre in
front of the Orangery is
bedded out in startling
colours as it was in
Victorian times, ringing
the changes each year, but
always incorporating a
maximum of contrast. In
the foreground is a circular
bed characteristically
mounded up to the central
Chusan palm with a pattern
of ageratums, scarlet
lobelias and the glaucous
rosettes of *Echeveria fulgens*
(syn. *E. retusa*).

Right: From the roof of the
house, the pattern of the
parterre beds in front
of the Orangery can be fully
appreciated. Flanked by
Irish yews (*Taxus baccata*
'Fastigiata'), they lead on to
a vista up the hill to the
Lantern (or Lanthorn)
Tower in the park, erected
as a folly in the early eighteenth century. [NM]

So many of the gardens shown in this book belong to great country houses, but the National Trust has some town gardens too. This is the rear garden of MOMPESSON HOUSE, built by Charles Mompesson in 1701 in the cathedral close at Salisbury in Wiltshire.

High-walled and largely overshadowed by the house in winter, the garden at Mompesson has challenges familiar to those who garden in towns – dank and cold in winter, hot and dry in summer – exacerbated here by the thin chalky soil. The layout is simple and unassuming with a central lawn and generous borders of old-fashioned flowers within a structure of compact acacias (*Robinia pseudoacacia* 'Bessoniana'). *Left*: The borders overflow with cottage-style flowers – Canterbury bells, shasta daisies, pinks and foxgloves.

Above: On the east side a pergola gives variety to the circuit walk. Furnished generously with climbers, it gives interest and colour through the year. *Clematis cirrhosa balearica* and *C. armandii* are followed by wisteria, *Clematis* 'Perle d'Azur' and honeysuckle, *Lonicera × americana*. Golden philadelphus planted within the pergola imbues it with a golden glow, especially on dull days. [NM]

Beatrix Potter's garden at HILL TOP in Near Sawrey, Cumbria. Using her paintings, old photographs and journals, the National Trust has restored the garden as an old-fashioned cottage plot.

Right: The long borders which flank the path up to the front door of the farmhouse contain a cottage-style mixture of flowers, vegetables and soft fruits. On the left is a rustic fence smothered with roses and honeysuckle and in the foreground the scarlet *Lychnis chalcedonica* clashes cheerfully with foxgloves and thalictrums. The onions have been allowed to run to seed, and further on there is a wigwam of sweet peas and a patch of the yellow loosestrife *Lysimachia punctata*.

Above: Jemima Puddle-Duck's rhubarb patch at Hill Top. On the left, the box beehive stands within a sheltered recess in the wall, known as a 'bee-bole'. [SR]

MOUNT STEWART in County Down
is one of the great gardens of Ireland,
created in the 1920s over an eighteenth-
century layout by Edith, wife of the 7th
Marquess of Londonderry. Taking advantage of the mild climate of the Ards
peninsula and vital shelter from the
established trees, she not only accumulated an astonishing collection of tender
and exotic plants from all over the world,
but also used her fertile imagination to
create a huge garden full of symbolism
and contrast.

One surprise is the Dodo Terrace, where
Lady Londonderry placed a menagerie of
cement creatures, some living, some
extinct, some mythical, relating to the
First World War and her Ark Club.
Members of the club, which included
family, friends and politicians, were given
the Order of the Rainbow (a symbol of
hope) and an animal name. Lord
Londonderry was commemorated by
Charlie the Cheetah because of his
prowess at cards, Winston Churchill
was Winnie the Warlock.

Left: The Dodo Terrace is glimpsed
from the Italian Garden, the main
parterre below the south front of the
house. The beds on this side of the
parterre contain plants of strong colouring combined with purple foliage. In
the foreground is a group of tender
South African *Watsonia pillansii* (syn. *W.
beatricis*) against violet-blue monkshood
and orange day lilies with spires of the
white form of *Veronicastrum virginicum*
behind.

From the formal gardens near the house
there is a dramatic transition to the soft
luxuriance of the Lily Wood, the shade
of the vine-covered pergola giving way
suddenly to a bright vantage point by the
sundial (*right*). Here are some of the
New Zealand flaxes, species and cultivars
of *Phormium*, part of the National Collection held by the garden. [SR]

In *Gardens of the National Trust*,   : 99 :
Stephen Lacey describes
MOUNT STEWART as 'a theatre
of imagery evoking family history
and Irish legend'. The Shamrock
Garden is set out in the three-
lobed shape of the shamrock leaf
with a topiary Irish harp in the
middle segment. It is delineated
by an enclosing hedge, now
regrown by the National Trust
in yew, surmounded by topiary
figures recounting an Irish
legend. At the heart of the
Shamrock Garden is the 'Red
Hand of Ulster', planted annually
with massed begonias. [SR]

MOSELEY OLD HALL in Staffordshire played a vital role in English history. In 1651, following his defeat at the Battle of Worcester, Charles II was on the run from his Roundhead enemies. He took refuge at Moseley before making his escape to France, disguised as a serving man.

When the National Trust took over Moseley in 1962, the garden was derelict. Graham Stuart Thomas collaborated with Christopher Wall, one of the Trust's Historic Buildings Representatives, to recreate a mid-seventeenth-century garden in tribute to Charles II's fortunate escape. This was to be the first of the Trust's historical garden reconstructions.

They based their Knot Garden on a scheme produced in the 1640s by the Rev. Walter Stonehouse for a Yorkshire garden. Simple, geometric designs were created in box, with gravels rather than the original ornamental plants within the box enclosures.

Left: A tunnel arbour was constructed in the style illustrated by Thomas Hill in his *Gardener's Labyrinth*, published in 1577. The arches of the arbour were made of oak, and planted with claret vines, *Vitis vinifera* 'Purpurea', *Clematis viticella* and *C. flammula*, with an underplanting of lavenders.

Right: On the south façade of the house a flower border was planted, using only plants in cultivation before 1700: hollyhocks, sweet peas, the original form of the corn marigold, *Chrysanthemum segetum*, and *Echium plantagineum*. [NM]

PECKOVER HOUSE is a late Georgian three-storey house in Wisbech, Cambridgeshire. The austerity of its front façade belies not only the exuberance of the interior, but also the style of the rear garden. Here can be seen an example of the 'garde-nesque' style, a term first proposed by John Claudius Loudon in 1832 to mean planting designed both to display the character of each plant and the art of the gardener.

Above left: Ribbon borders became fashionable as a Victorian expression of Italianate formality. Originally set out entirely in bedding plants, this one was designed by John Sales in the 1970s using a framework of permanent plants: London pride in contrast with the green of thrift and the silver-grey of cotton lavender. Bronze cordylines stand erect like pineapples above busy lizzies.

Below left: The broad gravel path to the Orangery is flanked by deep, matching borders, each opposite section with a different colour scheme, separated by pillars of roses and edged with alpine pinks. In the foreground, blue and white 'Headbourne Hybrid' agapanthus compete with Japanese anemones.

Above: The Summer Border at KNIGHTSHAYES COURT. This is situated close to the house, and its intricate pattern of yew hedges reflects the Victorian gothic of the fenestration. The scalloped shapes of the clipped yew bring down the scale from shrubs and tall herbaceous plants at the back, to the array of dwarf plants and alpines spilling onto the paving at the front: diascias, violas, erysimums, thymes, dwarf hebes, phloxes and pinks, with the blue grass *Festuca glauca* exploding among them. [SR]

The fuchsia tunnel at PENRHYN CASTLE in North Wales. The castle was built between 1822 and 1838 by Thomas Hopper for George Dawkins-Pennant. Hopper designed for his patron an enormous Norman castle, bristling with towers and battlements. Luckily this concept did not extend to the gardens, where the Gulf Stream provides a micro-climate in which orthodox plants may be used in unorthodox ways.

One example of this is the spectacular fuchsia tunnel on the lowest terrace of the walled gardens. An ironwork pergola, salvaged, repaired and re-erected by the Trust, stretches for 100m (330ft), with sixty hooped wrought iron arches. Thin metal cross-pieces run the entire length to provide rigidity, while thin green wire strung across from each upright supports lateral growth. Over this structure grows *Fuchsia* 'Riccartonii' (syn. *F. magellanica* 'Riccar-tonii') with delicate red flowers from mid-summer right through to the first frosts. It is supported by two clematis, purple *C.* 'Jackmanii Superba' and white *C.* 'Marie Boisselot' (syn. *C.* 'Madame le Coultre').

Although this is a substantial pergola, it is not dense, allow-ing visitors to enjoy views into the sunken garden below. [SR]

: 108 : Colchicums in the orchard at FELBRIGG HALL, Norfolk. The walled kitchen garden at Felbrigg, probably built in the 1740s by William Windham II, was restored by the National Trust after acquiring the property in 1972. Its original, labour-intensive style could not be sustained and had to be adapted to include more permanent ornamental planting while retaining as far as possible the character of a kitchen garden. In consultation with local staff and the head gardener, Ted Bullock, plans were drawn up by John Sales and implemented over a period. The gardeners train fruit trees along the walls, grow flowers and shrubs within box hedges, and cultivate grapes in the glasshouses and vegetables under cloches.

Alongside the vegetables, they also maintain the National Collection of colchicums, part of a nationwide scheme organised by the National Council for the Conservation of Plants and Gardens. Under this scheme, owners and managers of gardens undertake to conserve comprehensive collections of species and cultivars of a genus or otherwise defined group of plants. The scheme has proved an enormous success, with over six hundred national collections established.

The colchicum looks like a large autumn crocus, with its pale stem crowned by a single purple, mauve or white turban, rising straight out of the ground, devoid of leaves – they come later. They are in fact from a different family: the crocus is related to the iris, while the genus *Colchicum* is a member of the lily family. How the original stock of *Colchicum tenorei* reached Felbrigg is a mystery, though Ted Bullock holds to the theory that William Windham may have brought corms back from the Grand Tour, along with his collection of paintings and furniture. Whoever was responsible, the species thrived in the light, sandy soil, and is a wonderful sight in September.

Plentiful corms are naturalised in grass in the orchard, as shown here under an apple tree. This is their ideal habitat with the trees sheltering them from excessive heat. Asleep in summer, they begin to awake with the autumn rains, the blooms lasting from late August to early October. Thereafter the leaves appear, dying down in June.

Above: Colchicum speciosum 'Rosy Dawn'. [SR]

The National Trust is establishing orchards of traditional local varieties of apples right across the country, from Cotehele and Trelissick in Cornwall, to Nunnington Hall and Beningbrough Hall in Yorkshire, as well as holding special historic collections at places like Westbury Court in Gloucestershire and Erddig in North Wales. Apple Day in late October has become a popular date in the horticultural calendar.

Above: The apple orchard at BERRINGTON HALL, Herefordshire. The walled garden at Berrington is home to a collection of around fifty local, pre-1900 varieties of apples, put together by the National Council for the Conservation of Plants and Gardens. Some of the varieties date back several centuries, and the intention is that the orchard should provide part of a gene pool for the future, as well as giving interest and beauty to the visitor. This photograph shows 'Court of Wick' and in the background, 'Doctor Hare's'.

Top: 'Yellow Ingestrie' was raised around 1800 by Mr T.A. Knight of Elton Manor, Ludlow from a cross between 'Golden Pippin' and 'Yellow Pippin'. It is a mid-season variety of good flavour and attractive russet appearance.

Middle: 'Ashmead's Kernel' is a classic russet apple raised around 1700 and still in extensive cultivation because of its outstanding flavour; some say the best of any. It was raised by a Dr Ashmead in Gloucester and is a good West Country apple, if rather a light cropper. It keeps well and is ready to eat December to February.

Bottom: 'Madresfield Court' comes from the house and large garden of that name near Malvern in Worcestershire. It was raised by the head gardener, William Crump, early in the twentieth century, receiving an Award of Merit from the Royal Horticultural Society in 1915. It is an attractive apple, ready for eating between October and December.
[SR]

BERRINGTON HALL'S walled garden contains not only apples, but also medlars, figs, mulberries and quince trees. The wonderfully aromatic fruit of the quince is not easy to buy today, but was a favourite of cooks in Elizabethan and Stuart times when it was baked in pies, used in preserves and made into sweetmeats with honey and spices – the original name marmalade came from *marmelo*, the Portuguese for quinces. Here quinces are shown with an under-planting of rosemary and box (*left*).

Right: Crab apples, *Malus* 'Gorgeous' growing in the orchard at Berrington. [SR]

Right: The aster border at Upton House, Warwickshire. On the south-facing terraces, the asters are grown on the cool side of the brick wall of the vegetable garden. This is Upton's National Collection of a section of Michaelmas daisies, including the larger-flowered *A. amellus*; all highly resistant to mildew which so often disfigures the true Michaelmas daisies, the *novi-belgii* hybrids. Set effectively among contrasting drifts of grassy foliage, they are at their best in late September and early October.

Above: Detail of *Aster* × *frikartii* 'Jungfrau' at Upton. [SR]

Right: The parterre at WESTBURY COURT in Gloucestershire. The garden at Westbury was laid out by Maynard Colchester in the formal Dutch style that was the height of fashion in the last years of the seventeenth century, in the reign of William of Orange. The garden was designed to be useful and productive as well as beautiful and refreshing for its owners. Within a formal structure of walls, hedges, topiary and water, it combined vegetable production with flowers and fruit. Maynard Colchester's accounts show that he ordered bulbs including tulips, and these are to be seen in spring, along with the blossom of pre-1700 varieties of apple, plum and pear trees grown as espaliers or fan-trained along the walls.

In autumn, however, the formal plantings come into their own. In the parterre can be seen patterns of clipped box containing plantings of sage, lilies, and pot marigolds (*Calendula officinalis*), with cones and roundels of common box. In the background are Portuguese laurels *(Prunus lusitanica)*, and behind them, thorn trees and a massive tulip tree. [SR]

The low, flat water meadows of the River Severn provided Maynard Colchester with the vital ingredient for his Dutch-style garden: water. He built a long canal and a tall pavilion, from which his guests might look down on the formal layout of his parterres (*above*). [NM]

The garden at BODNANT in North Wales enjoys the most spectacular situation, set on a west-facing slope above the River Conway.

The estate was bought in 1874 by Henry Pochin, who proceeded to create a 'reposeful garden'. This was developed at the beginning of the twentieth century into a great garden by his grandson, the 2nd Lord Aberconway, building dramatic Italianate terraces and, with the help of plant hunters, amassing an unparalleled collection of Himalayan and Chinese plants, especially magnolias, camellias and rhododendrons, of which many important cultivars have been raised in the garden. Bodnant also holds the National Collection of embothriums.

The view from the top Rose Terrace looks towards the Carneddau range of Snowdonia, forming the magnificent backdrop to the garden. On the left is the eighteenth-century Pin Mill, brought from Gloucestershire and set up here in 1939. The 'Sunningdale Silver' form pampas grass dominates the foreground in October. [SR]

Overleaf: BODNANT is better known as a spring garden, but the autumn display is very fine. The brilliant tints of Japanese maple, *Acer palmatum* (left), the copper-coloured deciduous conifer, *Taxodium distichum* (beyond), and Tupelo *Nyssa sylvatica* (right foreground) contrast with the foliage of hydrangeas and rhododendrons. [SR]

: 122 : Autumn colour at SHEFFIELD PARK in Sussex. The garden is worth a visit at any season for the picturesque beauty of its landscape, its chain of lakes reflecting the grandeur of its specimen trees. It is particularly colourful in spring with rhododendrons reflecting pinks, whites and reds in the lakes, but it is in the autumn that the gardens become aflame. This rich overlay was applied by Arthur Soames, who bought the estate in 1909, but the framework of the garden had been built up by his predecessors, the Earls of Sheffield.

The 1st Earl at one stage sought the advice of the landscape designer, Humphry Repton. Repton remarked upon the vigour of the trees, 'Such is the power of vegetation at Sheffield Place that every berry soon becomes a bush, and every bush a tree, so that the natural shape of the vale is obliterated.' Lord Sheffield, however, was delighted by the vigour of his trees, and got on with the planting of his landscape without Repton's help.

This landscaping was continued by the 3rd Earl, who planted many of the conifers in the later nineteenth century, with the draining and extension of the four lakes. Arthur Soames followed by planting many of the deciduous trees that provide autumn colour, turning to red, orange and russet in contrast to the white pampas and large conifers. This photograph is taken from the Conifer Walk with *Acer palmatum* 'Osakazuki', *Aronia melanocarpa*, and *Cotinus* 'Flame' amongst the trees in their autumn dress.
[SR]

Details of some of the trees that provide autumn colour at SHEFFIELD PARK: Tupelo tree, *Nyssa sylvatica* (*right*); Sweet Gum, *Liquidambar styraci-flua* (*top*); Persian Ironwood, *Parrotia persica* (*above*). [SR]

: 126 : The Coronation Avenue at ANGLESEY ABBEY. As noted earlier (page 43), Huttleston Broughton, lst Lord Fairhaven, was devoted to royal anniversaries and avenues. Here he combined both, with an avenue of London planes and horse chestnuts planted to celebrate the coronation of George VI and Queen Elizabeth in 1937. Half a mile in length, this broad highway is a triple avenue of horse chestnuts. The original intention was to remove the horse chestnuts to make way for London planes, but just before the necessary trimming was due to take place, a ferocious storm broke up many of the planes and the long-term plan had to be re-adjusted. Some of the surviving plane trees are now in the car park, and others grace Swindon's town centre! [SR]

Neptune rising
out of the early
morning mist in
November at
WESTBURY
COURT.
He stands in a
T-shaped canal
completed
by Maynard
Colchester II,
nephew of the
man who laid
out the Dutch-
style gardens.
[SR]

Winter in the Cherry or East Garden at HAM HOUSE in Surrey. This was planted in 1975 to recreate the formal gardens that the Duke and Duchess of Lauderdale might have intended in the late seventeenth century. Their statue of Bacchus stands amid box-edged beds containing alternately dwarf cotton lavender (*Santolina chamaecyparissus* var. 'Nana') and Dutch lavender (*Lavandula angustifolia*), clipped annually to resemble pin cushions.

Running along the east and west sides of the Cherry Garden at Ham are tunnels of pleached hornbeam trained over iron hoops and underplanted with yew hedges. These are based on the tunnel arbours of sixteenth-century gardens (see also page 100), providing walks that gave shelter from the sun and showers, yet permitted cloistered views of the formal patterns. [SR]

Overleaf: Viburnum opulus berries at ANGLESEY ABBEY. Holly is not the only plant to provide vivid colour in mid-winter, and this viburnum – our native guelder rose – offers white flowers in June and autumn colours in October. There is also a yellow-berried form. [SR]

Left: The Old Garden at HIDCOTE. In spring and summer, the dominant colours are soft – blue, pink and mauve, with white and pale yellow (see pages 68–9), but on a frosty winter's day the garden is imbued with wonderfully subtle greys and browns. It is in this season that the clever architectural structure created by Lawrence Johnston is revealed.

Above: Having practised his growing passion for gardening in the Old Garden, Johnston's master-stroke was to have the courage to strike a long vista westwards to the sky, and to provide a succession of intriguing features along the way. [SR]

Overleaf: LYTES CARY in winter. Sir Walter Jenner's clipped topiary yews lead down to the 'dovehouse' at the end of the vista. It is, in fact, a water tower in disguise: a real dovecote would have kept the Elizabethans in fresh food through the winter months. [SR]

Left: The Winter Walk at ANGLESEY ABBEY. This was planted in 1998 to celebrate the centenary of the birth of the lst Lord Fairhaven. Designed by John Sales, then Head of Gardens, in collaboration with the head gardener, Richard Ayres, it replaced a derelict shelter belt, enriching an already extensive garden and offering an intriguing new route for winter visitors.

The Serpentine Walk is provided with a background of evergreens and arranged so that the visitor faces north to get the best out of the low, winter sun. Anglesey Abbey has always been strong on plants with attractive stems, and the Winter Walk follows this tradition with a range of maples, willows, kerria and dog-woods that are cut back hard to encourage fresh and colourful stems. *Cornus sanguinea* 'Winter Beauty' is a form of Britain's native hedgerow dogwood which is spectacular when planted *en masse* (*right*). [SR]

Halfway along a rich cavalcade of co-ordinated colour schemes is a restful circular space surrounded by the sweet-scented, October-flowering *Elaeagnus × ebbingei*. Around a statue commissioned to commemorate Lord Fairhaven is a simple arrangement of grasses, alternately *Stipa tenuissima* and *Festuca glauca*. [SR]

The Top Lake at SHEFFIELD PARK on a frosty morning. Winter is a time to enjoy the structure of trees, the infinite diversity of their branching and the subtle variations of colour and form revealed by the winter sun. Stem and bark effects also come into their own at this time, and at Sheffield Park this impact is doubled by the stillness of the mirror-like lake. Evergreens, especially conifers, are particularly telling in the low light. [SR]

POLESDEN LACEY in mid-winter. The view from the colonnade of the main house, with a statue of a griffin standing in the snow. [NM]

Stephen Robson

Stephen became interested in photography at art school, attending Goldsmiths' College in South London in the mid-1970s. He developed an interest in early photography and discovered the pictures of Eugène Atget. Atget's fabulous documentary series of urban Paris and the formal gardens surrounding it inspired him to explore his own surroundings with a camera. It was the man-made environment that interested him, rather than wild landscapes.

After college he worked for John Maltby, an architectural photographer, accompanying him with his ancient wooden Sanderson cameras and old Lancia sports car, photographing new buildings in London, such as the Barbican. In the 1980s he worked as a studio photographer, mainly for design agencies, but hankered after his own projects and working out of doors.

Returning to the subject of gardens in the 1990s meant learning again how to work with the effects of daylight on a subject which in itself is constantly changing through the seasons. Having worked in studios, it seemed natural to use large format cameras, and for long, wide shots Stephen likes to use a 5 x 4in camera with a 6 x 12cm film back. This gives an almost panoramic picture, which suits the subject but is very slow and cumbersome to use. However, he has increasingly used the 35mm camera, especially for close-ups with a macro lens. Stephen nearly always chooses Fuji film, generally preferring Provia F for a near to natural reproduction of colour.

His work for the National Trust has taken him to many of Britain's finest man-made landscapes and gardens. He particularly loves the spectacle of the great Cornish gardens in spring, when the magnolias flower among the bare, grey-green branches. This wave of spring then moves across the country and can be seen again weeks later in, say, the Lake District. However, it is not just the visual excitement of gardens that he appreciates. He also enjoys meeting the knowledgeable, and in many cases passionate gardeners. He often relies on them to help with the planning and captioning of the pictures, and owes a debt of thanks to them all.

Nick Meers

Nick was born in the Cotswolds and grew up in Gloucestershire and Dorset. His passionate love of the countryside started early, and a fascination with the landscape was consolidated after leaving school by travelling around New Zealand. The infinite grandeur of this landscape led him to give up sketching and watercolours in favour of grappling with a 35mm camera, and he graduated from the BA Honours course in photography at Guildford School of Art in Surrey.

He has worked on over thirty books about travel and landscape, including the first gardens book to be shot entirely in panoramic format. A commission for the National Parks in California that combined extreme scale with intimate details of landscape started him on an observation of how natural light changes, and its effects upon nature.

Almost exclusively, Nick uses Fuji film emulsions: for the soft light and vibrant colours found in British gardens, Fuji Velvia just cannot be beaten, with its superior grain structure and effortless handling of shadow detail. He uses a variety of medium and large format cameras. The Mamiya RB67 produces 6 x 7cm transparencies, and is a standard format for publishing, enabling instant proofing and various focal length lenses to be used. For pictures that contain gardens within an architectural context, he prefers to use a large format Linhof TechniKardan 5 x 4in monorail camera. This allows for lens corrections and multiple film formats, although the attendant equipment sometimes occupies more than one gardener's wheelbarrow. A fascination with the panoramic 'letterbox' format has led him to experiment with building his own cameras, combining the necessary architectural movements and choice of lenses within the panoramic format, a shape which some publishers have found exciting to use.

The major problem with using large cameras in gardens is their extremely slow speed both in the setting up, and in the making of pictures. He believes this to be an advantage, as the extra time spent setting up for a picture and waiting for ideal conditions usually produces more considered results. Patience is as an essential requirement for garden photography, as wanton flowerheads and quivering leaves, stirring in the inevitable breeze, require constant observation and swift reactions.

Nick has photographed gardens, architecture and landscapes for the National Trust for over fifteen years, relishing the demanding visual challenges that these commissions bring. He remains in debt to the hundreds of unnamed architects, engineers, designers and gardeners that have effectively done the hard work over the centuries for us all to enjoy.

Index